RESCHEDULED, NOT RELEASED

What Marijuana's New Status Really Means for Workers, Employers, and Public Safety

A Policy-Focused Analysis of Law, Regulation, and Public Safety

J THOMAS SMITH

First Edition

Disclaimer

This book is provided for informational and educational purposes only. It does not constitute legal advice, medical advice, clinical guidance, or regulatory compliance advice. Laws, regulations, and agency guidance may change over time. Readers are encouraged to consult applicable statutes, regulations, and qualified professionals regarding specific legal, medical, or compliance matters. The author disclaims any liability arising from the use of this material.

Notice Regarding Federal and State Law

Federal, state, and local laws governing controlled substances, workplace safety, and drug testing vary by jurisdiction and may change. Nothing in this book authorizes conduct prohibited by applicable law or regulation.

ISBN: 978-1-948034-10-4

Independently published

Printed in the United States of America

Table of Contents

Dedication

To the professionals who carry responsibility when others carry assumptions and to those whose commitment to safety, clarity, and accountability protects lives they will never meet.

Acknowledgments

This book reflects the contributions of many people and institutions whose work rarely attracts attention, but whose influence is felt every day in the systems that protect public safety.

I am grateful to the professionals working across transportation, healthcare, behavioral health, compliance, and regulatory oversight who continue to do their jobs with diligence during periods of uncertainty. Their commitment to prevention, consistency, and accountability provided the real-world grounding for this work.

I also acknowledge the educators, clinicians, supervisors, and administrators who have asked hard questions and insisted on clear answers. Their insistence on precision—especially when clarity was inconvenient—reinforced the need for this book.

My appreciation extends to colleagues in public mental-health systems, higher education, and professional certification bodies who have shaped my understanding of how policy, practice, and ethics intersect. Their work underscores the importance of standards that exist not merely on paper, but in daily decision-making.

Finally, I am grateful to those who understand that leadership during change is not about prediction, advocacy, or silence—but about responsibility.

Introduction

Why This Book Exists—and Why Timing Matters

When marijuana was announced as "rescheduled," the reaction was immediate—and predictable. Headlines moved faster than understanding. Conversations jumped straight to conclusions. For many readers, the word *rescheduled* sounded like permission.

This book exists because a gap opened between **what people think changed** and **what actually changed**—and in safety-sensitive environments, that gap carries consequences.

Rescheduling is a technical legal act. It does not rewrite workplace rules, erase regulatory authority, or grant behavioral permission. Yet misunderstanding has already placed careers, organizations, and public trust at risk.

This book restores clarity where assumption has taken hold.

Preface / Author's Note

Why I Wrote This Book Now

This book was written in response to confusion—not ideology. In the months following rescheduling announcements, I heard the same questions repeatedly from employees, employers, and compliance professionals.

I wrote *Rescheduled, Not Released* to close the gap between perception and authority, and to provide clarity during a moment when silence was being mistaken for permission.

"The law is reason, free from passion." — **Aristotle**

CHAPTER 1

What "Rescheduled" Actually Means—and Why So Many People Get It Wrong

When the federal government announced that marijuana would be rescheduled under the Controlled Substances Act, the reaction was immediate and, in many cases, misguided. Headlines declared a "historic shift." Commentators spoke as though a long-standing prohibition had quietly dissolved overnight. In workplaces, especially those governed by strict safety and compliance rules, conversations quickly turned from *what changed* to *what is now allowed.*

That leap—from classification to permission—is where confusion begins.

Rescheduling is a legal act, not a behavioral one. It is a technical determination about how a substance is categorized under federal law. It does not automatically change workplace rules, erase regulatory authority, or suspend existing safety standards. Yet many people interpreted rescheduling as a signal that marijuana had been functionally legalized, or at least normalized, across all contexts.

This chapter exists to slow that conversation down.

To understand what rescheduling actually means, it is necessary to separate three concepts that are often treated as interchangeable but are fundamentally different: **law**, **regulation**, and **permission**. When these concepts are blurred, individuals make decisions that feel reasonable but carry serious consequences.

Rescheduling Is a Classification Decision

Under the Controlled Substances Act, drugs are placed into schedules based on criteria such as accepted medical use, potential for abuse, and safety under medical supervision. Moving a substance from one schedule to another reflects a reassessment of those criteria. It does not, by itself, rewrite every statute, regulation, or policy that references that substance.

In practical terms, rescheduling marijuana to Schedule III acknowledges that it may have accepted medical uses and a different risk profile than substances classified in Schedule I. That acknowledgment is meaningful within medical, research, and pharmaceutical contexts. It may affect how the substance is studied, prescribed, or regulated in specific clinical environments.

What it does *not* do is grant blanket permission for use in all settings—particularly in environments where impairment, even at low levels, poses unacceptable risk.

Why the Public Reaction Was Predictable

The confusion surrounding rescheduling is not the result of bad faith. It is the result of how legal changes are communicated and consumed. Most people do not read statutes, regulations, or agency guidance. They rely on summaries, headlines, and social cues. When a change is described as "historic," it is reasonable for readers to assume it carries immediate practical effects.

But regulatory systems do not operate at the speed of headlines. They operate through formal processes, layered authority, and explicit implementation. A change in classification does not nullify existing regulations unless those regulations are formally amended. Until that happens, the old rules remain in force.

This distinction matters most in safety-sensitive environments, where rules are designed not around punishment, but prevention. In those settings, the question is not whether a substance is legal in some contexts, but whether its use is compatible with safety obligations.

The Cost of Assuming Permission

When people hear "rescheduled," many substitute the word "allowed." That substitution is rarely conscious, but it is powerful. Employees may assume that prior prohibitions no longer apply. Employers may hesitate to enforce policies they believe are outdated. Supervisors may avoid difficult conversations, fearing they are enforcing rules that no longer exist.

These assumptions can quietly erode compliance long before any incident occurs.

In regulated workplaces, especially those involving transportation, heavy machinery, or public trust, the consequences of misunderstanding are not theoretical. A single incorrect assumption can lead to job loss, regulatory action, or liability exposure—not because someone acted recklessly, but because they acted on incomplete information.

This is why clarity is not optional during periods of regulatory change. Silence creates space for assumption, and assumption fills that space quickly.

Why This Distinction Matters Going Forward

Rescheduling may eventually lead to regulatory updates. Agencies may revise guidance. Policies may be amended. But those changes occur through formal processes, not implication. Until rules are explicitly changed, they remain enforceable.

Understanding this is not about resisting change. It is about respecting how change actually happens in law and regulation. The most dangerous point in any transition is not the end state—it is the period in between, when old rules still apply but new narratives suggest otherwise.

This book is written for that in-between moment.

Chapter One establishes the foundation for everything that follows: rescheduling is real, but it is limited; meaningful, but not universal; and technical, not permissive. The chapters ahead will examine how this distinction plays out in specific regulatory systems, why public safety standards operate differently, and what responsibility looks like when clarity is in short supply.

Chapter One Summary

- Rescheduling is a legal classification decision, not a grant of permission
- Changes in drug scheduling do not automatically alter workplace rules or regulations
- Confusion arises when law, regulation, and permission are treated as interchangeable
- Assumptions during periods of change create risk for employees, employers, and the public
- Clarity—not silence—is essential when regulatory narratives shift

---

"The distinction between what is legal and what is permissible is the foundation of governance." — **Lon L. Fuller**

CHAPTER 2

Law, Regulation, and Permission: Why These Are Not the Same Thing

One of the most persistent sources of confusion in public discourse—especially during moments of legal change—is the assumption that *law*, *regulation*, and *permission* are interchangeable. They are not. Treating them as synonymous may feel intuitive, but it leads to errors that are costly in regulated environments and dangerous in safety-sensitive ones.

This chapter explains why those distinctions exist, how they function in practice, and why rescheduling marijuana has amplified misunderstandings that were already present long before any policy shift occurred.

Law Establishes Authority, Not Daily Practice

Law is the broadest layer of governance. Statutes passed by legislatures establish authority, define categories, and set outer boundaries. The Controlled Substances Act, for example, establishes schedules, enforcement powers, and federal jurisdiction over certain substances. When marijuana is rescheduled under that Act, the change occurs at the level of statutory classification.

But statutes are not instruction manuals. They do not govern daily operational decisions. They do not tell employers how to test, supervisors how to enforce, or professionals how to comply on a day-to-day basis. That work is delegated downward.

When people hear that "the law has changed," they often assume that daily rules have changed with it. In reality, law creates the *framework* within which more specific rules are written.

Regulation Translates Law Into Enforceable Rules

Regulations exist to operationalize statutes. Agencies are granted authority by law to write rules that specify how statutory goals are implemented. These rules are detailed, technical, and enforceable. They define procedures, standards, timelines, and consequences.

In safety-sensitive industries, regulations are intentionally conservative. They are built around prevention rather than reaction. The goal is not to determine fault after harm occurs, but to reduce the probability that harm will occur at all. This is why regulatory change is deliberate and formal.

Crucially, regulations do not change automatically when statutes are amended. Agencies must engage in rulemaking, which typically involves notice, comment, analysis, and publication. Until that process is complete, existing regulations remain in force—even if the underlying statute has evolved.

This is where many misunderstandings take root. A statutory change may be real and significant, but its regulatory implications are neither immediate nor implied.

Permission Is a Separate Question Entirely

Permission is the narrowest and most context-specific concept of the three. It answers the question, *"Am I allowed to do this, here, now?"* Permission is determined by applicable rules, policies, contracts, and conditions—not by general legal status.

For example, a substance may be legal under federal or state law, yet prohibited by workplace policy, licensing standards, or safety regulations. That prohibition is not symbolic. It is enforceable.

In regulated workplaces, permission is constrained by risk tolerance, not cultural norms. The fact that an activity is lawful in one context does not make it permissible in another. This is especially true where impairment—real or perceived—carries consequences beyond the individual.

Rescheduling has been widely interpreted as permission because the public conversation rarely distinguishes between these layers. But permission does not flow automatically from classification.

Why These Distinctions Matter More Than Ever

Periods of transition expose weaknesses in public understanding. When change occurs at the top of the legal hierarchy, people naturally assume it cascades downward. But in governance, cascades are controlled, not automatic.

Employees who rely on headlines rather than regulations may act prematurely. Employers who hesitate to enforce existing policies may expose themselves to liability. Supervisors who avoid clarity may unintentionally foster noncompliance.

None of these outcomes require bad intent. They require only misunderstanding.

The purpose of regulation is not to lag behind social change, but to ensure that change is integrated safely.

That integration takes time, analysis, and formal action. Until those steps occur, the absence of permission is not a moral judgment—it is a structural reality.

The Risk of Collapsing the Distinctions

When law, regulation, and permission are collapsed into a single concept, accountability becomes diffuse. People are unsure which rules apply, who enforces them, or when they change. In that uncertainty, informal norms begin to substitute for formal standards.

In safety-sensitive systems, informal norms are not a substitute for compliance. They are a liability.

This chapter reinforces a foundational principle that will recur throughout the book: **clarity is achieved by honoring distinctions**, not erasing them. Understanding where authority resides, how rules are implemented, and when permission exists is not pedantic—it is protective.

Rescheduling may signal evolving perspectives, but it does not erase regulatory structure. Until that structure is formally amended, permission remains governed by existing rules.

Chapter Two Summary

- Law, regulation, and permission serve different functions and operate at different levels
- Statutory changes do not automatically alter regulations or workplace rules
- Regulations translate law into enforceable, prevention-focused standards
- Permission is context-specific and often more restrictive than general legality
- Collapsing these distinctions creates risk, not flexibility

---

"Public safety is not a matter of convenience; it is a matter of trust." — **Learned Hand**

CHAPTER 3

Why Public Safety Is Different—and Always Will Be

Public safety operates under a different logic than most areas of law and policy. While many legal systems balance individual liberty against collective interest, public safety systems begin from a more constrained premise: **some risks are unacceptable, regardless of intent, legality, or social acceptance**.

This distinction is essential to understanding why changes in drug classification—even significant ones—do not translate easily into safety-sensitive environments. In these settings, the question is not whether conduct is lawful in the abstract, but whether it is compatible with the level of trust placed in those who perform critical functions.

Safety-Sensitive Roles and the Prevention Standard

Safety-sensitive positions are defined not by status, but by consequence. Pilots, commercial drivers, train engineers, pipeline operators, transit security personnel, and others entrusted with public welfare operate under a prevention-based standard. Their work is governed by the principle that harm must be prevented, not merely punished after the fact.

This is why public safety regulation emphasizes impairment, reliability, and judgment rather than intent. A safety system cannot wait for proof of misuse, recklessness, or wrongdoing. It must intervene at the point where risk becomes plausible.

In this context, the legality of a substance outside the workplace is secondary. What matters is whether its use introduces uncertainty into performance, reaction time, perception, or decision-making. Even marginal impairment—or the inability to reliably rule it out—can be disqualifying.

Why Zero-Tolerance Is Not About Morality

Zero-tolerance policies are often misunderstood as moral judgments. In public safety systems, they are not. They are **risk-management tools**.

These policies exist because safety-sensitive work leaves little margin for error. When consequences include loss of life, environmental damage, or large-scale disruption, regulators err on the side of prevention. This approach may feel strict, but it is grounded in responsibility rather than punishment.

Rescheduling does not alter this calculus. A substance's classification does not determine whether its effects are compatible with safety-sensitive performance. Regulators focus on detectability, duration, variability of effects, and the ability to establish reliable thresholds. Where those factors remain uncertain, prohibition remains the default.

The Role of Public Trust

Public safety systems depend not only on technical competence, but on trust. The traveling public assumes that those operating vehicles, infrastructure, and security systems are unimpaired and fully capable at all times. That assumption is not negotiable; it is foundational.

When trust is compromised—even by perception—the legitimacy of the system erodes. This is why public safety regulation often appears inflexible. Flexibility introduces ambiguity, and ambiguity undermines confidence.

Rescheduling may shift public attitudes, but it does not recalibrate the level of trust required in safety-sensitive roles. That requirement remains absolute.

Why Change Happens Slowly in Safety Systems

Safety regulation is deliberately conservative. Changes are tested, studied, and implemented gradually. This is not resistance to progress; it is recognition of consequence.

When regulators consider modifying standards, they evaluate not only scientific data, but operational realities: testing reliability, enforcement consistency, legal defensibility, and public acceptance. Until those elements align, maintaining existing standards is not inertia—it is prudence.

This explains why safety regulations often lag behind broader social or legal changes. The lag is intentional. It creates space for evidence, consensus, and infrastructure to develop before standards are altered.

Misunderstanding the Purpose of Safety Rules

A common error is to interpret safety rules as expressions of outdated values. In reality, they are expressions of **risk tolerance**. Safety systems are designed to minimize worst-case outcomes, not to reflect cultural trends.

This is why rescheduling, while meaningful in many contexts, does not compel immediate change in safety-sensitive regulation. The underlying question remains unchanged: *Does this substance introduce risk that cannot be reliably mitigated?*

Until the answer changes, the rules remain.

The Cost of Ignoring This Reality

When individuals or organizations treat public safety rules as negotiable, they expose themselves to consequences that feel disproportionate. Enforcement actions, job loss, and public scrutiny often follow—not because of malice, but because safety systems respond to risk decisively.

Understanding that public safety operates under a different logic is not pessimistic; it is protective. It allows individuals and employers to navigate change without missteps and to respect the boundaries that exist for a reason.

This chapter underscores a central theme of the book: public safety is not a subset of general policy—it is its own domain, governed by its own imperatives.

Chapter Three Summary

- Public safety systems operate under a prevention-based standard
- Safety-sensitive roles are defined by consequence, not legality
- Zero-tolerance policies manage risk rather than express moral judgment
- Public trust is foundational and non-negotiable
- Regulatory change in safety systems is intentionally slow and deliberate
- Rescheduling does not alter the core logic of public safety regulation

---

"Regulation exists not to punish, but to prevent the harm that cannot be undone." — **Felix Frankfurter**

CHAPTER 4

DOT Drug Testing: What Hasn't Changed—and Why That Matters

Few areas illustrate the gap between public perception and regulatory reality more clearly than drug testing under the authority of the U.S. Department of Transportation. Following announcements about marijuana rescheduling, questions flooded in from employees and employers alike: *Does this change DOT testing? Are positive tests still violations? Does medical or recreational legality matter now?*

The short answer remains unchanged. The longer answer explains why.

DOT Authority Is Regulatory, Not Cultural

The Department of Transportation's drug and alcohol testing program exists for a single purpose: to protect public safety. It is not designed to reflect social trends, state-level legalization, or shifting public opinion. Its authority flows from federal regulation, not cultural acceptance.

DOT drug testing is governed by detailed regulations that define who is tested, how tests are conducted, how results are reviewed, and what consequences follow. These rules apply uniformly across covered safety-sensitive positions and do not change unless formally amended through the federal rulemaking process.

Rescheduling marijuana under the Controlled Substances Act does not amend DOT regulations. Until DOT publishes new rules, existing standards remain fully enforceable.

What DOT Tests For—and Why That Has Not Changed

DOT testing panels are not symbolic. They are selected based on substances that pose unacceptable risk in safety-sensitive functions. Marijuana remains on that panel not because of ideology, but because of unresolved issues related to impairment, detection windows, and reliability.

Unlike alcohol, marijuana metabolites can remain detectable long after acute effects have subsided. Regulators have not established a scientifically reliable threshold that distinguishes impairment from past use across diverse individuals and conditions. In the absence of such a threshold, zero-tolerance remains the only defensible standard.

Rescheduling does not resolve this problem. Classification affects how a substance is regulated under federal law, not how it behaves in the human body or how reliably impairment can be measured.

Medical Marijuana and DOT Testing

One of the most persistent misconceptions involves medical marijuana. Employees often assume that a physician's recommendation or state authorization provides protection under DOT rules. It does not.

DOT regulations make no exception for medical marijuana. Medical Review Officers are prohibited from verifying a positive test result as negative based on a medical marijuana authorization. A verified positive remains a violation, regardless of state law or medical purpose.

This is not a matter of discretion. It is a regulatory requirement.

CBD Products and the Risk of Assumption

CBD products present a related, and increasingly common, source of confusion. Many are marketed as non-intoxicating and legal, leading users to assume they are safe from a testing perspective. That assumption is risky.

CBD products are not uniformly regulated. Some contain trace amounts of THC sufficient to trigger a positive test. DOT guidance has repeatedly warned that use of CBD products does not excuse a positive marijuana test result.

Rescheduling does not alter this guidance. Employees who rely on product labeling rather than regulatory standards assume risk that the system does not absorb on their behalf.

The Role of Medical Review Officers and SAPs

Medical Review Officers (MROs) and Substance Abuse Professionals (SAPs) operate within strict regulatory boundaries. Their roles are often misunderstood as discretionary or advisory. In reality, their authority is defined by regulation.

MROs verify test results according to federal rules. SAPs evaluate and recommend treatment or education following violations. Neither role includes the authority to waive violations based on legality, medical use, or rescheduling status.

This structure exists to ensure consistency and defensibility. Allowing case-by-case exceptions would undermine uniform enforcement and expose the system to legal challenge.

Why This Clarity Protects Everyone

Clear, uniform enforcement protects employees, employers, and the public. It removes ambiguity, limits arbitrary decision-making, and ensures that safety standards are applied consistently.

Confusion about DOT drug testing often arises not because the rules are unclear, but because people expect them to change in response to external developments. DOT regulations are not reactive. They are precautionary.

Until DOT regulations are formally amended—and there is no automatic trigger for such amendments—marijuana remains prohibited for DOT-regulated safety-sensitive employees. That reality is not political. It is procedural.

Understanding this protects careers. It protects organizations. And most importantly, it protects the public.

Chapter Four Summary

- DOT drug testing is governed by federal regulation, not cultural trends
- Rescheduling marijuana does not change DOT testing requirements
- Marijuana remains a prohibited substance for DOT-covered employees
- Medical marijuana authorizations do not excuse positive DOT test results
- CBD products carry risk and do not provide protection
- MROs and SAPs must follow regulation, not discretion
- Uniform enforcement preserves safety, fairness, and legal defensibility

---

"Assumptions are the termites of policy." — **Henry Kissinger**

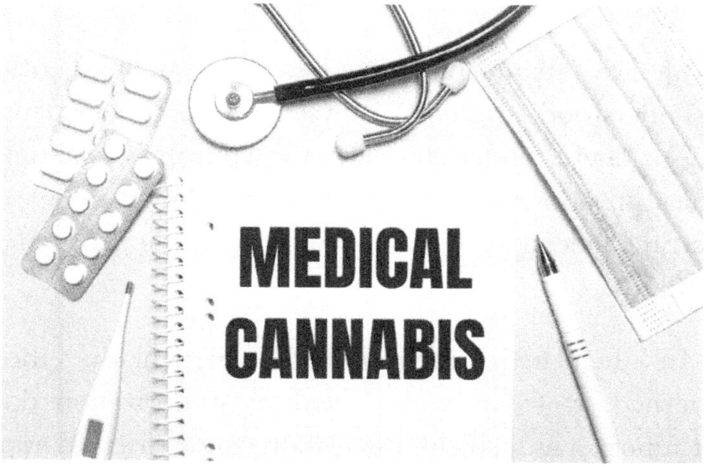

CHAPTER 5

Medical Marijuana, CBD, and the High Cost of Assumptions

Few topics generate more confusion in regulated workplaces than medical marijuana and CBD. The confusion is understandable. These products are widely marketed, increasingly normalized, and often framed as therapeutic or benign. Yet in safety-sensitive and regulated environments, assumptions about their permissibility can be costly.

This chapter addresses why legality, medical authorization, and product labeling do not equate to permission—and why relying on those assumptions places individuals and organizations at risk.

Medical Authorization Is Not Regulatory Immunity

Medical marijuana occupies a unique and often misunderstood space. A physician's recommendation may be lawful under state law and appropriate within a clinical relationship. But that authorization does not override federal regulation, workplace policy, or safety standards.

In regulated environments, particularly those governed by federal rules, medical authorization does not function as a shield. Regulations are written to apply uniformly, regardless of individual circumstance. This uniformity is intentional. It ensures that safety standards are consistent, predictable, and legally defensible.

When employees assume that a medical authorization confers protection, they misinterpret the scope of that authorization. Medical permission operates within the bounds of healthcare law. Regulatory compliance operates within a different framework altogether.

The Problem of Impairment Versus Presence

A central challenge in marijuana regulation is the distinction between impairment and presence. Unlike alcohol, where impairment can be measured with relative precision, marijuana testing detects metabolites that may remain in the body long after acute effects have subsided.

This creates a regulatory dilemma. Safety systems cannot rely on subjective assessments of impairment, nor can they assume that presence is harmless. In the absence of a reliable, universally applicable impairment threshold, regulators default to prevention.

Rescheduling does not resolve this scientific challenge. Until testing can reliably distinguish impairment from historical use in a way that is enforceable and defensible, zero-tolerance remains the operative standard in safety-sensitive contexts.

CBD: Legal Does Not Mean Risk-Free

CBD products are frequently marketed as legal, non-intoxicating, and safe. These claims contribute to a false sense of security among users. In reality, CBD products are not uniformly regulated, and their composition can vary widely.

Some CBD products contain trace amounts of THC sufficient to trigger a positive drug test. Product labels are not guarantees. Even well-intentioned consumers may be exposed to risk through contamination, mislabeling, or variability in manufacturing.

Regulatory systems do not evaluate intent. A positive test result is assessed based on outcome, not expectation. Employees who rely on product claims rather than regulatory standards assume risk that the system does not absorb.

Employer Policies and the Illusion of Flexibility

Employers often face pressure to adapt policies in response to evolving social norms. In some industries, flexibility may be appropriate. In regulated or safety-sensitive environments, flexibility is constrained by external authority.

An employer cannot authorize conduct that violates federal regulation. Even where discretion exists, exercising it without clear regulatory support can expose organizations to liability. Policies that appear compassionate may inadvertently create inconsistency, undermine enforcement, or erode safety culture.

Clear policies protect everyone. They remove ambiguity, set expectations, and reduce the likelihood of misunderstandings. When policies align with regulation, enforcement feels less personal and more procedural.

The Human Cost of Misunderstanding

The consequences of assumption are often borne by individuals. Employees may lose jobs they believed they were allowed to keep. Careers can be disrupted not by misconduct, but by misinterpretation. These outcomes feel unjust to those affected, yet they are often predictable within the regulatory framework.

This is why clarity matters. Employers and regulators have a responsibility to communicate boundaries clearly, especially during periods of change. Silence or ambiguity invites assumption, and assumption invites harm.

Why Restraint Remains Necessary

Rescheduling reflects evolving perspectives on marijuana's potential uses. It does not eliminate the unresolved issues that make regulation challenging in safety-sensitive environments. Until those issues are addressed through evidence, rulemaking, and infrastructure, restraint remains the prudent course.

This is not a rejection of change. It is an acknowledgment of responsibility.

Chapter Five Summary

- Medical marijuana authorization does not override regulatory or workplace rules
- Presence of marijuana metabolites is not equivalent to impairment, but remains regulated
- CBD products carry testing risk despite legal marketing claims
- Employers cannot authorize conduct prohibited by regulation
- Assumptions about legality create personal and organizational harm
- Clear communication and restraint protect safety and fairness

---

"Systems fail not when rules exist, but when they are misunderstood."

Donella H. Meadows

CHAPTER 6

The Cost of Getting It Wrong: Careers, Liability, and Public Trust

Regulatory misunderstanding rarely announces itself loudly. More often, it accumulates quietly—through assumptions, half-answers, and informal interpretations—until a consequence makes it visible. In the context of marijuana rescheduling, those consequences are already emerging, and they are not abstract.

This chapter examines what happens when individuals and organizations misinterpret regulatory boundaries, and why the costs of getting it wrong extend beyond any single employee or employer.

Career Consequences Are Often Irreversible

For employees in regulated or safety-sensitive positions, the margin for error is narrow. A single positive test result can trigger mandatory removal from duty, referral to a Substance Abuse Professional, and a structured return-to-duty process. In some cases, employment ends entirely.

These outcomes are not disciplinary in the traditional sense. They are procedural. Once a violation occurs, the system responds according to predefined rules. Intent, belief, or misunderstanding does not alter that response.

Many individuals who experience these consequences report feeling blindsided. They believed that legality, medical authorization, or rescheduling insulated them from risk. The system, however, does not evaluate belief—it evaluates compliance.

This disconnect is not merely unfortunate; it is preventable.

Employer Liability Does Not Disappear With Rescheduling

Employers sometimes assume that legal change reduces their exposure. In regulated environments, the opposite is often true. Periods of transition increase scrutiny. Enforcement agencies expect employers to maintain standards, communicate clearly, and apply rules consistently.

Failure to do so can result in findings of noncompliance, civil penalties, or adverse outcomes in litigation. Policies that are unclear, inconsistently enforced, or informally relaxed create evidentiary problems when incidents occur.

An employer who tolerates noncompliance—intentionally or inadvertently—assumes risk that cannot be transferred. Rescheduling does not dilute that responsibility.

The Ripple Effect on Organizations

Beyond individual cases, misunderstanding erodes organizational culture. When rules appear negotiable, employees test boundaries. Supervisors hesitate. Compliance becomes uneven. Over time, this undermines the credibility of safety programs.

Restoring that credibility after an incident is far more difficult than preserving it through clarity. Organizations that navigate change successfully do so by reinforcing expectations, not relaxing them in response to ambiguity.

Public Trust Is Fragile—and Easily Lost

Public safety systems rely on trust that is rarely visible until it is compromised. The public assumes that safeguards are in place, that standards are enforced, and that risk is managed proactively.

When incidents occur that reveal gaps in enforcement or understanding, trust erodes quickly. Even isolated failures can have outsized impact, shaping perception far beyond the immediate facts.

This is why regulators emphasize consistency. The legitimacy of safety systems depends on predictable enforcement, not discretionary accommodation.

Why "Everyone Is Confused" Is Not a Defense

A common refrain during periods of change is that confusion is universal. While true, it is not exculpatory. Regulatory systems assume that those operating within them bear responsibility for understanding applicable rules.

This may feel harsh, but it reflects the stakes involved. Safety-sensitive roles carry obligations precisely because misunderstanding has consequences beyond the individual.

The responsibility to seek clarity rests with both employees and employers. Where guidance is unclear, the safest assumption is restraint.

Clarity as Risk Management

The costs outlined in this chapter are not inevitable. They arise when clarity is absent and assumptions fill the gap. Clear communication, training, and policy alignment are forms of risk management.

Organizations that invest in clarity reduce the likelihood of violations, protect their workforce, and preserve public trust. Individuals who seek authoritative guidance before acting protect their careers.

Rescheduling may continue to evolve. Regulatory frameworks may eventually adapt. But until those adaptations are explicit, the cost of getting it wrong remains high.

Chapter Six Summary

- Regulatory misunderstanding can result in permanent career consequences
- Employer liability persists—and may increase—during periods of change
- Inconsistent enforcement undermines organizational safety culture
- Public trust depends on predictable, uniform standards
- Confusion does not excuse noncompliance
- Clarity functions as a critical risk-management tool

"Leadership is not revealed in comfort, but in moments of uncertainty." — **John C. Maxwell**

CHAPTER 7

Leadership in the Gap: Employer Responsibility During Regulatory Change

Periods of regulatory change place unusual pressure on leadership. Rules may remain formally intact while narratives suggest otherwise. Employees look for signals. Supervisors seek reassurance. Silence is often mistaken for flexibility, and ambiguity for permission.

This chapter addresses the responsibility of leadership during that gap between announcement and implementation—and why restraint, clarity, and consistency are essential tools when certainty is in short supply.

The Gap Between Announcement and Enforcement

Regulatory systems rarely change overnight. Announcements precede implementation, and implementation follows formal process. During this interval, the rules that exist remain enforceable, even as public perception shifts.

For employers, this gap is hazardous. Employees may assume that leadership's silence reflects acquiescence. Supervisors may hesitate to enforce policies they believe are outdated. Informal norms can begin to replace formal standards.

Leadership during this period is not about prediction. It is about **reaffirmation**.

Why Silence Is Interpreted as Permission

In organizational settings, silence is rarely neutral. When expectations are not restated, they are reinterpreted. This is especially true when external narratives suggest change.

Employees rarely seek to violate policy intentionally. More often, they look for cues. When those cues are absent, they fill the gap with assumption. That assumption, once shared, can spread quickly.

Clear communication interrupts that process. It reminds employees that rules remain in effect until formally changed. It reframes enforcement as procedural rather than discretionary.

Policy Alignment as a Leadership Obligation

Employer policies must align with applicable regulations. During periods of change, this alignment should be reviewed, not relaxed. Policies that mirror regulatory language provide clarity and defensibility.

Updating policies prematurely—before regulatory change is formalized—creates exposure. Conversely, reaffirming existing policies demonstrates stability and respect for process.

Leadership does not require certainty about the future. It requires fidelity to the present.

Training and Communication Matter More Than Ever

During regulatory transitions, training becomes a preventive tool. Briefings, written notices, and supervisor guidance can prevent misunderstandings before they harden into behavior.

Effective communication during these periods shares three characteristics:

- It is clear about what has **not** changed
- It avoids speculation about future changes

- It emphasizes where authoritative guidance will come from

This approach builds trust, even when answers are incomplete.

The Risk of Selective Enforcement

One of the most damaging responses to uncertainty is selective enforcement. When rules are applied inconsistently—whether out of sympathy, hesitation, or misunderstanding—organizations undermine their own standards.

Selective enforcement creates inequity, invites challenge, and erodes morale. It also weakens an organization's position if enforcement later becomes necessary.

Consistency is not rigidity. It is fairness.

Leadership as Stewardship

Leadership during regulatory change is an act of stewardship. It involves protecting employees from avoidable harm, safeguarding organizational integrity, and maintaining public trust.

This stewardship requires courage. It may involve enforcing unpopular rules. It may require repeating messages that seem redundant. It may require resisting pressure to move faster than the regulatory system allows.

But these actions serve a larger purpose. They ensure that when change does arrive, it is integrated responsibly rather than reactively.

Chapter Seven Summary

- Regulatory change creates a gap between announcement and implementation
- Silence during this gap is often interpreted as permission
- Leadership must reaffirm existing rules until formal change occurs
- Policies should align with regulation, not speculation
- Training and communication reduce risk and confusion
- Consistent enforcement preserves fairness and trust
- Leadership during uncertainty is an act of stewardship

"Change is inevitable. Confusion is optional." — **Alvin Toffler**

CHAPTER 8

What May Change—and What Will Not

Rescheduling marijuana signals that change is possible. It does not specify when, how, or in what contexts that change will occur. This distinction is critical. Anticipating change is not the same as operating as though it has already happened.

This chapter clarifies what kinds of changes may reasonably occur over time, what is unlikely to change, and why responsible systems prepare without presuming outcomes.

What May Change

Over time, regulatory systems may adapt to new evidence, technologies, and consensus. In the context of marijuana, several developments are possible.

First, research may continue to clarify the relationship between use, impairment, and risk. Improved testing methods could eventually distinguish reliably between recent impairment and historical presence. If such tools emerge and are validated, regulators may reconsider existing standards.

Second, agencies may engage in formal rulemaking. This process is deliberate and transparent. It involves public notice, comment, analysis, and publication. Any resulting changes will be explicit, documented, and enforceable. They will not occur by implication.

Third, employer policies outside regulated environments may evolve. In contexts where safety-sensitive obligations are lower, organizations may choose to adapt rules to reflect changing norms or workforce expectations. These decisions, however, remain bounded by applicable law and risk tolerance.

Each of these developments requires time. None are automatic consequences of rescheduling.

What Will Not Change

Certain principles are unlikely to shift, regardless of classification.

Public safety standards will remain prevention-focused. Where risk cannot be reliably mitigated, restriction will persist. Trust placed in safety-sensitive roles will continue to demand high levels of reliability and accountability.

Regulatory authority will remain hierarchical. Statutes enable regulation; regulation governs practice. Permission will continue to be context-specific and conditional.

Most importantly, compliance will remain an affirmative responsibility. Individuals and organizations will continue to be expected to know and follow applicable rules, even during periods of transition.

The Danger of Acting Ahead of Change

One of the most common errors during periods of anticipated reform is acting as though reform has already occurred. This impulse is understandable, but risky.

Premature action exposes individuals to enforcement under existing rules. It exposes employers to liability. It creates inconsistency that is difficult to unwind once formal change arrives.

Responsible systems prepare quietly. They monitor developments, review policies, and plan for possible adaptation. They do not substitute expectation for authority.

Preparing Without Presuming

Preparation does not require prediction. It requires awareness.

Organizations can prepare by:

- Monitoring official agency guidance
- Reviewing policies for alignment with current regulation
- Training leadership on how to communicate uncertainty responsibly

Individuals can prepare by:

- Seeking authoritative information
- Asking compliance-based questions
- Avoiding reliance on informal sources

This posture allows adaptation without exposure.

Why This Moment Still Matters

Rescheduling has already changed the conversation, even if it has not yet changed the rules. That shift creates both opportunity and risk. Opportunity lies in improved understanding, research, and dialogue. Risk lies in assumption and premature action.

This book exists to help readers navigate that moment responsibly.

Change will come, or it will not. Either way, clarity remains the safest policy.

Chapter Eight Summary

- Rescheduling opens the possibility of future regulatory change
- Meaningful change occurs through formal rulemaking, not implication
- Improved testing and research may influence future standards
- Core public safety principles are unlikely to change
- Acting ahead of formal change creates risk
- Preparation should be deliberate and evidence-based
- Clarity remains essential during periods of uncertainty

"The life of the law has not been logic; it has been experience."
— Oliver Wendell Holmes Jr.

Conclusion

Clarity Is the Safest Policy

Periods of change test systems not because the future is uncertain, but because the present becomes misunderstood. Marijuana rescheduling has created such a moment—one in which perception has moved faster than regulation, and assumption has filled the space where clarity should reside.

Throughout this book, one principle has guided the analysis: rescheduling is not release. It is not permission.

It is not an instruction to behave differently in environments governed by safety, trust, and prevention. It is a legal classification decision whose implications unfold slowly, deliberately, and through formal process.

For individuals, the lesson is straightforward but demanding. Responsibility does not pause during periods of transition. Acting on headlines rather than authority exposes careers to avoidable risk. Seeking clarity before acting is not caution—it is professionalism.

For employers and leaders, the responsibility is broader. Silence is not neutral. Ambiguity is not compassionate. During periods of regulatory uncertainty, leadership requires reaffirming standards, communicating clearly, and enforcing rules consistently. These actions protect not only organizations, but the people within them.

For public safety systems, the stakes remain unchanged. Trust must be preserved. Risk must be managed proactively. Standards must remain defensible, even when they are unpopular. These imperatives do not bend easily to cultural momentum, nor should they.

This book has not argued against change. It has argued against confusion. Change that arrives through evidence, rulemaking, and infrastructure can be integrated responsibly. Change assumed into existence creates harm before it creates benefit.

As conversations about marijuana policy continue to evolve, clarity must remain the anchor. Clear rules, clear communication, and clear understanding are not obstacles to progress—they are prerequisites for it.

In the end, safety is sustained not by speed, but by discipline. Not by assumption, but by authority. And not by silence, but by clarity.

Conclusion Summary

- Rescheduling is a legal classification, not a behavioral directive
- Acting on assumption during transition creates avoidable harm
- Individuals retain responsibility for understanding applicable rules
- Employers must lead with clarity, consistency, and restraint
- Public safety systems prioritize prevention over adaptation speed
- Change must be explicit to be integrated safely
- Clarity remains the most reliable form of protection

"What we know matters. How we know it matters more." —
Daniel J. Boorstin

Notes and References

Controlled Substances Act, 21 U.S.C. § 801 et seq.

49 C.F.R. Part 40 — Procedures for Transportation Workplace Drug and Alcohol Testing Programs

49 C.F.R. Parts 382, 655, and related modal regulations

U.S. Department of Transportation, Office of Drug & Alcohol Policy & Compliance guidance and notices

Administrative Procedure Act, 5 U.S.C. § 551 et seq.

Final Regulatory Clarification

Marijuana Rescheduling and DOT Compliance

(Status at Time of Publication)

As this book was finalized for publication, the federal government announced that marijuana would be rescheduled from Schedule I to Schedule III under the Controlled Substances Act. This development has generated widespread public confusion—particularly among safety-sensitive employers, transportation professionals, and regulated employees—regarding whether marijuana use is now permitted in federally regulated workplaces.

This section clarifies what has changed, what has not changed, and why the central thesis of this book remains fully intact.

What Changed

- Marijuana has been reclassified to Schedule III under the Controlled Substances Act.
- Schedule III substances are recognized as having accepted medical use under federal law and a lower potential for abuse than Schedule I substances.

This change reflects a shift in drug scheduling, not a change in workplace safety law.

What Did Not Change

Despite the rescheduling, no changes have been made to drug-testing or enforcement requirements issued by the U.S. Department of Transportation.

Specifically:

- Marijuana remains a prohibited substance for all safety-sensitive employees regulated by the DOT.
- DOT drug-testing panels still include marijuana (THC).
- A verified positive marijuana test remains a violation of federal safety regulations.
- There is no medical marijuana exception under DOT rules.
- State legalization laws do not override federal DOT authority.

These requirements continue to be enforced across all DOT-regulated agencies, including:

- Federal Motor Carrier Safety Administration
- Federal Aviation Administration
- Federal Railroad Administration
- Federal Transit Administration
- Pipeline and Hazardous Materials Safety Administration

What Employers Must Still Do

DOT-regulated employers are still required to:

- Maintain federally compliant drug-testing programs
- Test safety-sensitive employees for marijuana
- Remove employees from safety-sensitive functions after verified positive results
- Refer employees to a qualified Substance Abuse Professional (SAP)
- Complete all Return-to-Duty and Follow-Up testing requirements

Failure to enforce these obligations may expose employers to regulatory penalties, liability exposure, and safety risks.

Common and Dangerous Misinterpretations

The rescheduling of marijuana has led to several incorrect assumptions that place employers and workers at risk:

- "Rescheduled means permitted" — False
- "Medical marijuana is allowed under DOT rules" — False
- "State legalization overrides federal safety law" — False
- "Employers may relax enforcement" — False

None of these interpretations are supported by federal transportation regulations.

Why the Thesis of This Book Remains Unchanged

The title of this book—RESCHEDULED, NOT RELEASED—captures the precise legal reality now confronting employers and regulated employees.

Rescheduling alters how a substance is categorized under federal drug law.

It does not eliminate safety obligations, testing authority, or enforcement power.

Until DOT regulations themselves are formally amended, marijuana use remains incompatible with safety-sensitive transportation duties, regardless of state law, prescription status, or public perception.

The law has shifted categories.

It has not shifted responsibility.

Forward-Looking Note

Any future changes to DOT policy would require formal rulemaking, published guidance, and agency-specific implementation. Until such changes occur, employers and employees must comply with existing regulations—not speculation, headlines, or social media interpretations.

This clarification reflects federal guidance current as of the date of publication.

About The Author

Dr. J Thomas Smith is a nationally respected authority on mental health, addiction, and drug policy whose work bridges clinical science, federal law, media, and public education. A licensed mental health professional, board-certified addiction counselor, attorney, award-winning broadcaster, and Telly Award–winning documentary film producer, Dr. Smith brings a rare, multidisciplinary perspective to conversations where policy, psychology, and lived experience intersect.

Dr. Smith's academic foundation spans behavioral science, psychology, counseling, and law. He earned a Bachelor of Science from the University of the State of New York (now Excelsior University) and a Master of Science in Counseling Psychology from Vermont College of Norwich University. He holds a Doctor of Philosophy (PhD) in Behavioral Science from Universidad De San Jose, with specialization in mental health and addictionology, and a Doctor of Psychology (PsyD) from California Coast University. He also earned a Juris Doctor (JD) from Texas Southern University's Thurgood Marshall School of Law, providing formal legal training in statutory interpretation, regulatory analysis, and public policy.

Professionally, Dr. Smith holds multiple licenses and national credentials, including Licensed Professional Counselor (LPC), Licensed Chemical Dependency Counselor (LCDC), National Certified Counselor (NCC), Certified Clinical Mental Health Counselor

(CCMHC), and Master Addiction Counselor (MAC). He is an attorney licensed in multiple jurisdictions. He has served on national committees for the National Board for Certified Counselors and the American Mental Health Counselors Association, contributing to ethical standards, assessment practices, and professional accountability across the behavioral health professions.

Dr. Smith's clinical career has focused extensively on substance use disorders, co-occurring mental health conditions, trauma, and populations affected by stigma, criminalization, and systemic barriers to care. He is widely recognized for translating complex neuroscience, regulatory frameworks, and statutory language into clear, human-centered guidance—always emphasizing patient dignity, public safety, and evidence-based treatment.

In parallel with his clinical and legal work, Dr. Smith has had a distinguished career in media and public education. As an award-winning radio announcer, he leveraged broadcast media to inform and elevate public understanding. He also co-hosted Counseling Today with Tom Clawson, the longtime Executive Director of the National Board for Certified Counselors, bringing counseling ethics, professional issues, and mental health policy into national conversation. His work as a Telly Award–winning documentary film producer reflects his commitment to education, historical accuracy, and social impact through storytelling.

As federal drug policy evolves, Dr. Smith has emerged as a leading voice clarifying the essential distinction between rescheduling and legalization. His expert analysis of marijuana's reclassification to Schedule III under the Controlled Substances Act emphasizes what the change recognizes—medical utility under federal regulation—and what it does not permit—unrestricted use or federal legalization.

Through his writing, filmmaking, broadcasting, and speaking, Dr. Smith advocates for policies rooted in clarity rather than confusion, compassion rather than punishment, and science rather than fear. RESCHEDULED, NOT RELEASED reflects his core mission: ensuring that conversations about drugs, mental health, and reform remain honest, responsible, and centered on the people most affected by policy decisions.

Speaking And Training Inquiries

For keynote presentations, trainings, or expert briefings on marijuana rescheduling, mental health, addiction policy, or related subjects, Dr. J Thomas Smith is represented by Salem Speakers Bureau.

Email: support@salemspeakers.com

Call or Text: 312-667-7473

More information: https://salemspeakers.com/dr-j-thomas-smith/

Made in the USA
Monee, IL
04 November 2026

67382291R00039